THE S

ᴜʟ

SITTING BULL

BEING

A FULL AND COMPLETE HISTORY OF THE NEGOTIATIONS
CONDUCTED

Which resulted in the Surrender of Sitting Bull and his entire Band of
Hostile Sioux in 1881.

A Vivid Description of Indian Life, and Thrilling Adventure, written by
Scout Allison, in his own Graphic Style.

BY

SCOUT ALLISON

[Edward H. "Fish" Allison]

1891

Contents

PUBLISHER'S NOTES

Edward H. "Fish" Allison (1847 – 1918) was also known as Henry West. He is listed in the War Department records of 1883 as a scout. In 1880, he had already helped negotiate with the Lakota leader, Gall, who had fought Custer at the Little Bighorn, to bring his people into Standing Rock Reservation.

On May 20, 1889, Allison filed two applications for an army disability pension, listing both of his names but in reverse order on the separate applications. On both applications, he listed service in Company D, 10th Ohio Cavalry and Company K, U.S. 22nd Infantry. The 22nd served in Dakota Territory at the time Allison was there. Both forms carry the same application number and certificate number. There are several renewals of this certificate in subsequent years, always listing both names, and showing him to be an "army invalid." The pension over the years was $6 to $10 per month.

Allison spent time in veteran hospitals. On the National Home for Disabled Volunteer Soldiers record it indicates he was admitted September – October, 1891, June, 1896 – February, 1897, and December 26, 1899 – January 23, 1900, and records his age in 1900 as 44, which is incorrect.

Whoever filled in the form apparently couldn't do math because they listed his enlistment in the 10th Ohio as being in 1862 with service until July, 1865. If he was 44 in 1900, he served from the time he was six until he was nine. In fact, he was 53 in 1900 and had served in the Civil War from the age of fifteen to eighteen.

At the time of his discharge in 1900, he gave his occupation as "scout," his marital status as "single," and his next of kin as "friend: Colonel J.D. Platt." James Platt was a prominent Dayton, Ohio businessman and a veteran of the 10th Ohio Cavalry in the Civil War, having served as captain (brevet lieutenant-colonel) of Company D. Allison appears in the roster of the 10th Ohio as Henry A. West, age 18 at discharge.

Allison gave his "Residence Subsequent to Discharge" as Fort Pierre, South Dakota.

1

Under Kind and Degree of Disability in the Civil War it states "GSW [gunshot wound] r. shoulder."

He is listed in the 1916 Indian census as living on the Rosebud Reservation, SD. Allison died on May 19, 1918 at the Battle Mountain Sanitarium, National Home for Disabled Volunteer Soldiers. That facility was in Hot Springs, SD and is today a National Historic Landmark for its architecture and history. Allison is buried in Hot Springs National Cemetery. His effects were sent to a grandson named Edwin Allison in Wagner, on the Yankton Indian Reservation.

BUREAU OF AMERICAN ETHNOLOGY

CATALOGUE OF MANUSCRIPTS

NO. 1755

SURRENDER OF SITTING BULL

E.H. ALLISON

1897

MANUSCRIPT AND NOTES

In September, 1933, the Chief of the Bureau of American Ethnology turned over to the writer the Manuscript of E.H. Allison, requesting that the manuscript be checked against contemporary records and documents with a view to determining its authenticity, truthfulness, and accuracy.

The information specifically desired was: Was Allison the person he claimed he was; did he do the things he claimed that he did; and if so, was the narrative set forth in his manuscript a true and accurate account of the events leading up to the surrender of Sitting Bull.

The original manuscript was checked against contemporary records and documents, and found to be truthful, authentic and accurate.

This work was completed and filed with the Bureau of American Ethnology October 11, 1933.

John G. Carter.

TO AN HONEST MAN

GENERAL WILLIAM P. CARLIN,

U. S. ARMY.

THIS VOLUME IS RESPECTFULLY INSCRIBED BY

ONE IN WHOM HE BELIEVED.

THE AUTHOR.

William Passmore Carlin (1829 – 1903) was a career Army officer (West Point graduate, 1850) from Illinois. He served in the Civil War, including leadership roles at Chickamauga, Chattanooga, the Atlanta campaign, and Sherman's March to the Sea. After the war he served in the west.

PREFACE

In the history of the United States, there are few names more familiar to the reading public, than that of Sitting Bull, whose surrender, ten years ago, attracted, in the United States and Canada, universal attention, and the event was not unnoticed by the nations of the Old World. It having been my good fortune to be chosen by the U. S. Military authorities, to conduct the negotiations for the surrender of the wily old chieftain and his formidable band of warlike Sioux, it becomes apparent that I alone could write a correct history of that event, and hardly a day passes that I am not asked why I don't write the matter up for publication. To these questions I would usually reply, that perhaps someday I would, and this publication is made in fulfillment of that promise, and in response to what seemed to me like a public demand. I trust it will be received by the American people in a charitable and kindly spirit. But mine enemies may laugh in "ghoulish glee," for I have written a book.

Very truly,

E. H. A.

In the summer of 1880, Cox & Floweree, owners of the "Circle F" brand on the Sun River Range, in Montana, determined to drive a large herd of cattle down the Milk River Trail for shipment at Bismarck, Dakota. It was a dangerous undertaking, for the Milk River Valley was known to be the hunting ground of the hostile Sioux, who after the battle of the Little Big Horn, had taken refuge in the North-West Territory. On the other hand, the excellent grazing, together with an abundance of wood and water, were considerations that outweighed any apprehensions of danger from savages. Accordingly a bunch of twelve hundred head of steers were rounded up, and started down the Milk River Trail, handled by twelve cowboys, in charge of J. R. Cox, one of the owners, and Will Floweree, son of the other member of the firm, with Bill Norris as guide, and a colored man, who was cook and teamster, in charge of the solitary mess wagon.

Probably referring to G.R. "Bill" Norris, one of Montana's early ranchers. William Floweree, at that time 19-years-old, was the son of Daniel Floweree, who had come to Montana during the 1860s gold rush. His prospecting luck allowed him to afford to bring Texas longhorn cattle up the Chisholm Trail in 1865. By 1880 the Floweree operation was running somewhere between 25,000 and 40,000 head of cattle. The town of Floweree and Floweree Butte are named for him. Young Will was later a Montana State Senator.—Ed. 2018

When the outfit reached Fort Belknap, and were about to enter territory of uncertain hospitality, I was engaged to accompany them as Interpreter. Before accepting the position, 'however, I exacted from every member of the party, a promise of strict obedience to my orders in the event of meeting, or having any trouble with Indians. The extent of what was considered hostile country was more than three hundred miles in length, embracing the entire valley of the Milk River to its confluence with the Missouri, and about one hundred miles of the Missouri Valley, from the mouth of Milk River to the Military Post of Camp Poplar River, which at that time was garrisoned by two companies of the 11th U. S. Infantry, with Captain O. B. Reed in command.

Civil War veteran Ogden Benedict Read (1843 – 1889) previously served at Fort Custer, which was built after the Little Bighorn disaster. He and the 11th Infantry were transferred to Poplar River in 1880. Sadly, he shot himself on April 15, 1889 at his home in New York, leaving a wife and three children. This was apparently due to financial difficulties and an ongoing murder trial involving a close friend.—Ed. 2018

Leaving Fort Belknap, we proceeded down the Milk River by easy stages, driving only about ten miles a day, and had reached a point near the mouth of Frenchman's Creek, at ten o'clock, on about the first of August, 1880, when we found ourselves completely surrounded by savages, evidently preparing to attacks They occupied every hilltop and eminence within a radius of about one thousand yards, and numbered three hundred and fifty warriors, while there, were about seventeen of us. Many of our party were in favor of immediately opening fire upon the Indians, hoping thus to turn them away. Such action would have been worse than madness. The moment had come for me to act. First reminding the men of their promise to obey my orders, I directed them to go about making camp for dinner, as if nothing unusual had happened, and put up the cook tent as usual. I ordered two of the men to partially round up the herd, while four or five men were ordered to lie down in a careless attitude, and lounge on the grass in plain view of the savages, and by all means, I cautioned no one to make any show whatever of alarm. I explained to the men, that I would ride out and meet the Indians, and would then act as circumstances required. That I would probably invite a few of the head chiefs to come and have dinner with me, and repeated the caution, that if they saw me returning, accompanied by any number of savages, to be sure and maintain an appearance of calm indifference. I then selected the largest group of savages and rode at an easy canter toward them, carrying Winchester resting across my saddle bow. Drawing near to the Indians, I hailed them with the Sioux greeting, "*How, mi ta ku ya pi!*" (Hail, my kinsmen!) "I am glad to find myself once more among friends. Is my brother, The Gall, with you?"

"Yes." they replied; and immediately an Indian left the group in search of Chief Gall, with whom he soon returned. The Gall, with whom I had been acquainted for many years, exhibited some surprise at meeting me, and, after a friendly handshake, he asked me if "that herd of cattle belonged to me." I had had no time for an elaborate preparation for the interview, no time to formulate answers to possible questions that I would be required to answer, and here was one at the very outset, to which I must unhesitatingly reply. Quick as thought, as if by inspiration, the answer sprang from my lips, "No; they belong to the Queen of England. They have been purchased by her for her army."

That reply saved the lives of seventeen men, my own included, and it saved to the owners of the Circle F Brand twelve hundred head of cattle. I went on to tell The Gall, that an agent of the Queen had bought the cattle, and knowing that I was a master of the Sioux language, and a friend of the Sioux Indian, had employed me to see that the herd was safely conducted through the Milk River Valley; that in anticipation of our meeting some of the friends of the Queen—the Sioux—the agent had provided me with two caddies of tobacco and a quantity of sugar and coffee, as an offering for them, as a token of friendship and esteem, and that I wanted The Gall to select twelve leading warriors and accompany me to the camp, where the men were preparing dinner for them, after partaking of which, they would receive the tobacco, sugar and coffee to be distributed to the warriors.

I hardly think The Gall believed my story, but it might be true, and having taken refuge on British soil, it would not do to molest persons or property under the protection of the British government. His countenance showed plainly that he was disappointed, but he accepted with good grace my invitation to dinner, and alter selecting twelve warriors, included in the invitation, he ordered the others to raise the siege, and repair to a place of rendezvous on the Milk River, half a mile distant.

Returning to the camp with the thirteen Indians, I informed our party of what had transpired. Dinner was soon ready, and our savage guests fell to and ate as only Indians can. Dinner over, the tobacco, sugar and coffee were taken from the wagon and formally presented by me to Chief Gall, as the representative of his people. This done, the twelve took their departure, The Gall alone remaining

8

to hold further Converse with me. It was at this interview that I conceived the idea of visiting Sitting Bull's camp, with a view to bring about his surrender to the U. S. authorities. I intimated as much to The Gall, and solicited his aid, promising that if I succeeded through his assistance, he should be recognized as chief of that band. He made no promise at the time, but invited me to visit their camp, which he said was at Ruined Timber, a mountain jungle, about twenty miles from Woody Mountain, where was a trading post and a small garrison of Canadian troops, adding that he would return with his band in a few days to Canada, where I would find him if I visited the camp. We shook hands and -parted, and soon we saw the entire band of three hundred and fifty warriors, as they filed by our camp, on their way to the Buffalo Range in the foot hills of the Little Rocky Mountains.

Gall (c. 1840 – 1894) was a Hunkpapa Lakota battle leader. He played an important role in the victory of the Sioux and Cheyenne at the Little Bighorn against Custer. After submitting to life on Standing Rock Reservation, he farmed and was a jurist on the Court of Indian Affairs. He became friends with Indian Agent, James McLaughlin, whose memoir is an important source for Custer scholars. Gall attended the reunion of 7th Cavalry officers at Little Bighorn in 1886, ten years after the battle. Years later, in answer to endless questions about "who killed Custer," Gall explained that there was so much smoke, dust and excitement, no one could tell who anyone was.—Ed. 2018

A LONESOME RIDE

I continued with the herd until it reached Fort Buford, Dakota, on about the first of September, when, the danger being past, and there being no longer any need of my services, I severed my connection with the Cattle Company, and presented myself to Major David H. Brotherton, in command of the Fort, to whom I reported the facts set forth above, regarding my interview with Chief Gall, and communicated to him my plan for bringing Sitting Bull and his people into Fort Buford.

David Hammet Brotherton (1831 – 1889) was a career officer and West Point graduate (1854).—Ed. 2018

He recognized the practicability and probability of success of my plan, and seized the opportunity of securing to himself the honor of receiving the surrender of the famous chieftain, and immediately authorized me to begin the work, by starting at once for Sitting Bull's camp, leaving me to conduct the negotiations in such manner as circumstances and my own judgment might dictate.

I lost no time in preparation, and the following morning found me on the way to Ruined Timber, distant from Fort Buford about two hundred and thirty miles. My route lay along the Missouri, west from Fort Buford about ninety miles, sixty-five miles to Camp Poplar Creek, and twenty-five miles from that place to Wolf Point, where I turned away from the Missouri, on a line due north, for Woody Mountain, in Canada. Here I had to cross a plain, one hundred and ten miles wide, without wood and but little water. The entire distance seems to be one vast, undulating plain. But in fact, from the moment I left the Missouri Valley, I began the ascent of the Woody Mountain, for in reality, the northern edge of this plain forms the summit of the Woody Mountain Range. I met with no adventure in the two days occupied in crossing. It was altogether a lonesome journey. The only thing noticeable was the total absence of any kind of game whatever. My thoughts were fully occupied with the work I had undertaken. The chances of success or failure, the danger awaiting me, when I should attempt to enter the inhospitable precincts of the camp of the reputed savage and hostile chief. But I had no thought of turning back. For twenty years the U. S. Government had vainly tried to bring these same Indians into the Agencies. Every possible means had been employed. Famous Indian diplomats, priests, preachers, lawyers, and whole armies had been in turn employed to effect the capture or surrender of Sitting Bull, costing millions of dollars, and hundreds of human lives; but Sitting Bull, with his formidable band of Hunkpapa Sioux were still on the war path, still a menace and terror to the pioneers of the plains, and I had undertaken to do that which had baffled all others. It was the one opportunity of my life, and I determined to succeed or perish in the attempt. The sun was almost down, on the evening of the fourth day out from Fort Buford, when I reached the northern extremity of the plain, or, as it is sometimes called, "the jumping-off place." Here I found myself on the summit of Woody Mountain Range. The sky was clear, and the time—evening—favorable for making observations.

Aided by an excellent pair of field glasses, I scanned the northern slope of the range, and the valley below, but for a long time could discover no traces of either Indians or Whites. Finally, when the night shades began to lower, a faint, cloud-like appearance became visible, forming over what seemed to be a little valley, lying between-two spurs of the mountain, and distant about fifteen miles. Training my glasses upon the spot, I could discern in the gathering darkness, objects that had the appearance of cloud shadows on the hillside, and moving down into the valley. I had found the camp. The dark objects on the hillside were the Indians driving in their pony herds for the night. The cloud like appearance was smoke, which the still night air held suspended over the valley.

After carefully noting the direction, I set out on foot, leading my horse, determined to reach the camp that night. The difficulty of the task can only be realized by one who has himself traversed a mountain jungle; but I got through. About two o'clock in the morning, passing over the brow of a long low ridge, I came in view of the camp, laid out in an irregular zigzag fashion, along the banks of a small mountain stream. Light was shining through many of the canvas tepees, where fires were still, at that late hour, burning brightly within. Many of the Indians had not yet retired, and a low murmur was audible, the hum of human voices reaching where I stood regarding the scene below. I. halted on the ridge just a moment, to breathe and to think of something to say that would aid me in securing a friendly reception. There were many Indians in the camp whom I had known, and some whom I had personally befriended years before, when they had visited the Trading Post on Grand River, in Dakota. Others were there whom I had known at Cheyenne River and Standing Rock Agencies, before they were starved by thieving Indian Agents, into leaving the Agencies to join Sitting Bull.

"How would they receive me?" was the all-important question with me just then. But I had little time for reflection. Mounting my horse, I rode at a rapid walk towards the camp. I had approached within about thirty steps of the outer line of tepees, when I was discovered by an Indian watchman, who came rapidly toward me, his rifle in his hands, ready for use. I reined in my horse and awaited his approach. He came and stood by my horse, and looking up through the darkness, asked, "Who are you, and where did you come from?" I replied by asking, "Where is The Lung's tepee?" He repeated his question. I then told him that I was a friend of The Lung, that I had come to visit him, and inquired again for his tepee. He partly turned his face away and muttered, "I wonder who it is? Whoever he is, he speaks our language," and then turning to me, he said, pointing to a tepee, only about fifty steps away, "That is The Lung's tepee." "That's where I'm going," said I, and giving my horse the rein, I was soon at the door of The Lung's tepee. Dismounting, and taking the end of my lariat in my hand, the other end being attached to the horse, I went into the lodge, Indian fashion, without the ceremony of knocking.

I found The Lung and his wife still up, and I was given a hearty welcome. Mrs. Lung immediately set about preparing something for me to eat, while The Lung plied me with questions about his relatives at the Agencies in Dakota. But he did not have me long to himself. In less than five minutes, the tepee was crowded full of Indians who wanted news of their friends from across the line. I gratified their wishes to the best of my ability; but in the midst of the interview, I heard my Indian name (*Ho gahu*, which means Fish) called by someone outside, by whose voice I recognized Chief Gall. I responded promptly by going out, where I found that the glowing fire within had so blinded my eyes that I could discern nothing; but a little way off I heard the voice of The Gall, saying, "Come this way," and as I approached him, groping my way through the darkness, he added, "I'm going to kill you."

"That's easily done" I replied, "I'm here alone, and there are a thousand of you. But if you want a deed done worthy of record, why don't you have me killed by one of your little boys, or by a squaw; surely, it would not be an act of bravery for you to kill me." He laughed, and said, "Come with me." I followed him to his lodge, where I was provided with a good supper, consisting of boiled buffalo tongue, a kind of fried cake and coffee. My horse, too, was cared for by some of the Gall's followers. I stayed in the camp three days, during which time I was not favored with an audience with Sitting Bull, who chose to ignore my presence in the camp. But I accomplished much during this first visit to the hostiles. I kindled in their minds, a desire to go back to their old hunting ground, by contrasting, most unfavorably, their condition as fugitives in a strange land, with that of their friends, living peacefully in their own country, under the protection of the U. S. Government. I fully succeeded in persuading Chief Gall to come in and surrender with his entire following, which was nearly two-thirds of the whole tribe, and he sealed the compact by presenting me with a fine horse, and when I started on my return, he accompanied me for nearly twenty miles, and when we finally parted, he promised to meet me on the Missouri River, with all his following and their families, in twenty-two days. I considered the work well begun, with great promise of ultimate success, and hastened back to Fort Buford, where I submitted an official report to Major Brotherton, who I found in a very unhappy mood, occasioned by a communication from Department Headquarters.

BROTHERTON REBUKED

After Major Brotherton had sent me to the hostile camp, he reported his action to General Terry, Department Commander, and had received a reprimand for sending a man on so important a mission, without first consulting higher authority, making it impossible for Major Brotherton to act any further in the premises.

Alfred Howe Terry (1827 – 1890) was a distinguished Civil War veteran and a respected non-West Point general. It was Terry who commanded the 1876 Yellowstone Expedition that resulted in Custer's death. See The Terry Diary: Battle of the Little Bighorn.—Ed. 2018

He told me, however, that he would telegraph my report to Gen. Terry, who, he thought, would order the work continued. But I had found two telegrams and a letter, on my return to Buford, from Gen. Wm. P. Carlin, who was in command of the Military Post, near Standing Rock Agency, Dak., requesting me to come to him, as he was in great need of my services. I was in a quandary. My mind was filled with conflicting emotions. I felt somewhat piqued at General Terry's needless interference, yet I wanted to go on with the work. On the other hand, General Carlin, whom I esteemed more than anyone I knew, and to whom I felt under obligations, having been Interpreter for him for five years, was in need of my services, and again, there was my agreement to meet Chief Gall. My course was determined by the arrival of the Steamboat *Batchelor*, on its way down the Missouri. Here was an opportunity to go to Bismarck, within fifty-five miles of Gen. Carlin's Post, and I took passage; greatly to the disappointment of Major Brotherton, who begged me to stay, at least till he could wire my report to Gen. Terry.

The Batchelor *was captained at this time by legendary riverboat man, Grant Marsh. In June, 1876, Marsh had piloted the steamer* Far West *on a record-breaking trip down three rivers carrying the wounded survivors of Custer's defeat from the mouth of the Little Bighorn to Fort Lincoln. The biography of Marsh is an important source document for Custer scholars.—Ed. 2018*

There was a telegraph line between Buford and Bismarck, with a station at Fort Stevenson, at which place I was met by a Messenger with a telegram from Major Brotherton, notifying me to look out for a telegram from Gen. Terry, in Bismarck. Landing at Bismarck, I found the following telegram awaiting me.

Headquarters Department, of Dakota Fort Snelling, Minn.,

Oct. 16, 1880.

Mr. E. H. Allison, Bismarck, Dak. Await in Bismarck further orders from this office.

A. H. TERRY,

Brig. Gen. Com'dg Dept, of Dak.

There was a Military telegraph line, connecting Bismarck with Standing Rock, by which I wired Gen. Carlin a brief statement of the work begun, and Gen. Terry's telegram, and submitted the matter to him, for his decision, as to what I should do. He wired me "That however much he needed my services," the interests of the government would be best served, if I could effect the surrender of Sitting Bull, and advised me to place myself under Gen. Terry's orders. I accordingly waited further orders from Department Headquarters, which in consequence of the wires being down, east of Bismarck, did not reach me until the 20th, when a dispatch came, as follows:

Headquarters Department, of Dakota Fort Snelling, Minn.,

Oct. 20, 1880. Mr. E. H. Allison, Bismarck, Dak.

Sir:—You will proceed with all possible speed, back to Fort Buford, where you will find specific instructions awaiting you. Relays of horses have been placed on the road.

A. H. TERRY.

Brig. Gen. Com'dg.

The distance from Bismarck to Fort Buford was two hundred and forty-five miles, which I made in a little less than thirty five hours, changing horses eleven times. Reaching Buford, I found Maj. Brotherton restored to cheerfulness by the successful termination of his efforts to have me continue the work which gave so much promise of finally putting an end to a long and disastrous Indian war.

Before setting out on a second visit to the hostiles, and, in as-much as I was now acting under authority that could not be disputed. I deemed it prudent, absolutely necessary in fact to demand certain conditions to be observed, and strictly enforced by the Military Authorities in that Department. First, that I should be left free to act on all occasions, as my own judgment should dictate. Second, that I should receive full and unqualified support in any measure that, in my judgment, became necessary. Thirdly, that no movement of troops in the field should be made without my knowledge and approval. Receiving assurance that these conditions would be observed, I made careful and deliberate preparations for my second visit to the hostiles. I had a wagon loaded with provisions, consisting of hard bread, sugar, coffee, bacon, and tobacco. I selected four of the best mules in the Quartermaster's stables, to draw the wagon. Private Day, Co. E, 7th Infantry, volunteered as teamster, dressed in citizen's clothes. Many of the old timers at the Fort tried to dissuade him from going with me, declaring that he would never come back - alive: that it was only the act of a madman to take an outfit like that into the hostile camp. That if I wanted to go alone and sacrifice myself to Indian treachery, why, well and good; but I had no right to sacrifice Day, and four good Government mules; but Day was a brave man, and proof against their solicitations.

There was a Lieutenant Russell Day of the 6th Infantry at Fort Buford during this period.—Ed. 2018

A CHAPTER REPLETE WITH STIRRING EVENTS

It was about the 25th of October, 1880, when we pulled out front Buford, reaching Camp Poplar Creek in two days, where I was met by an Indian runner from Bull's camp sent with a message to me front Chief Gall, to the effect that I would find him, with the entire camp, at the mouth of Frenchman's Creek, on the Milk River, about one hundred and fifty miles from Poplar Creek. Accompanied by the runner, whose name was Strong and, we proceeded on our journey, making only about twenty miles a day. When we had reached within about six miles of the camp, we came upon a lone tepee, erected on a small mound near the trail; an old squaw stood near, observing our approach. Riding up to her, I learned that her son, who was in the tepee, had, the day before, quarreled with another Indian in the camp, over a horse trade, and that her son had killed the other Indian, and he was now, in compliance with the Indian custom, when guilty of the shedding of blood, performing an act of purification. She also informed me that during the preceding night, their Indian enemies, the Blackfeet, had made an attack on the camp, and had succeeded in running off twenty-six head of horses, without, however, doing any other damage, and that a war party was on their trail. This was most unwelcome news. The camp was sure to be in an uproar, and the warriors in a frame of mind, anything but favorable to my purpose; but this was mild intelligence compared with what we were about to witness in the next forty-eight hours.

About three o'clock, p.m., we reached the camp, which was on the west bank and near the mouth of Frenchman's Creek, when I was rather agreeably surprised, and somewhat puzzled, by receiving a pressing invitation, which could easily be construed into a command, to make my home at Sitting Bull's lodge, as long as I stayed in the camp. I accepted the invitation, but stipulated that Chief Gall should superintend the distribution of the provisions which I had, brought them. To this Sitting Bull readily acceded, and notwithstanding the turbulent condition of the camp, I was soon comfortably housed, together with the soldier, in the tepee of the great Indian Priest and Prophet, Sitting Bull. After an early supper, I sought and obtained a private interview with Chief Gall, who informed me that he had resolved to effect the surrender of the entire band, Sitting Bull and all, but to accomplish this, more time would be required than he had first anticipated. He must first go back to Canada, to enable Sitting Bull to keep an engagement to meet Major Walsh, of the Dominion forces, in a council, at the Woody Mountain Trading Post. And to insure success, and expedite matters, he advised that I should meet him again at Woody Mountain, as soon as possible, after reporting to Major Brotherton, at Fort Buford. Considering the circumstances, I deemed it best to acquiesce in his plans. Yet I was anxious to make some kind of a showing on this trip, that would encourage Major Brotherton, and reward him for the confidence he had placed in me. I explained this to Chief Gall, who told me to remain in the camp two days, to rest my mules, and by that time he would have twenty families ready to send in with me; but he cautioned me not to let Sitting Bull know their real purpose, but to lead him to suppose they were only going in to the Agency on a visit to their friends.

Perfectly satisfied with these arrangements, I returned, a little after dark, to Sitting Bull's lodge, where the soldier, who could not speak a word of the Indian language, was having rather a lonesome time of it, and was growing somewhat anxious for my safety. We were both very tired, and soon lay down to rest, while I engaged the old Chief in conversation. Sitting Bull's family at that time consisted of his two wives, (sisters), two daughters, and three sons, the eldest being a daughter of seventeen, the other daughter being next, about fourteen, the eldest son, Crow Foot [1873 – December 15, 1890], since dead, seven years old, and the two youngest boys were twins, born about three weeks before the battle of the Little Big Horn, and were, therefore, not more than four and a half years old; one of the twins was named *Ih-pe-ya-napa-pi*, from the fact that his mother "fled and abandoned" him in the tepee, at the time of the battle.

The accompanying cut shows the arrangement of beds, etc., in the lodge, while we were there.

18

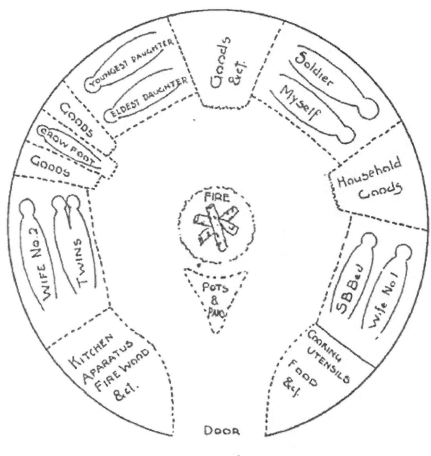

SITTING BULL'S LODGE.

I continued in conversation with Sitting Bull until about midnight, when I fell asleep.

I must have been asleep less than an hour, when I was awakened by the sharp crack of a rifle ringing out on the still night air, and the simultaneous war whoop of contending savages. The camp was instantly in a state of the wildest confusion. Indian women, seizing their babes, fled, screaming, they knew. not wither, for safety; warriors suddenly awakened from their slumbers, seized their arms and flew with the speed of the wind to the aid of their comrades, who were already engaged in conflict with an enemy, whose presence could only be determined by the sharp report and flashes of fire from their guns, as they fired in the darkness upon the Sioux

19

camp. Here was an opportunity for the soldier and myself to prove our friendship, by aiding the Sioux warriors in their defense of the camp, which we proceeded to do, by seizing our rifles and hastily joining the warriors, who, by this time, had turned the enemy, whose firing soon ceased altogether, and we all returned to the camp, where comparative quiet was restored; but no one slept anymore that night. The fact that myself and companion took part in the defense of the camp, was favorably commented on by all, and in all probability saved our lives, for the Indians are very superstitious, and their blood was up; something was wrong; in fact, things had been going wrong for several days. There must be a "Jonah" in the camp, and how easy it would be to find a pair of "Jonahs" in the persons of the two white men in camp; but our prompt action had made a most favorable impression, and diverted their thoughts from the subject of "Jonahs," and I improved the opportunity by comparing their uncertain, hunted existence with the happy life of their friends at the Agencies in Dakota, whose wives and little ones were even then sleeping peacefully in their beds, without fear of being disturbed by prowling bands of Indian foes.

A number of warriors followed cautiously after the retreating Blackfeet, but failed to come up with them. They returned to camp about ten in the morning, and reported finding blood-stained bandages on the trail, so there must have been some of the enemy wounded. Among the Sioux, no one was hurt, nor did they lose any horses on this occasion. But danger was yet lurking near. About two in the afternoon, a warrior came into camp, and reported the discovery of a small herd of buffalo, about four miles from camp. About thirty warriors mounted their horses and went out to kill them; among the number was Scarlet Plume, a popular young brave, who was a favorite with everyone. The warriors approached the buffalo under cover, till they were within easy rifle range, when they opened fire and killed all but one, which struck out across the plain, seemingly unhurt. Young Scarlet Plume alone gave chase, following the animal and finally killing it near the head of a ravine running up from the Milk River which at that point was densely studded with timber. He had killed his last buffalo. He was alone and more than a mile from his companions. A party of Blackfeet braves, concealed in the timber, had been watching his movements, and now while he was busily engaged skinning the buffalo, they approached, under cover of the ravine, shot him, took his scalp, and made good their escape. His body was found by his father, Old Scarlet Thunder, and was brought by him into camp, a little before sunset that evening. Then indeed, there was weeping and wailing in that camp. Language utterly fails me when I try to describe the scene that followed. His old mother, his five sisters, and scores of friends and relatives tore their hair, slashed their limbs with knives, till the ground where they stood was wet with hot human gore, rent their garments, calling in a loud wailing voice upon the name of the lost son and brother.

RETURN TO BUFORD WITH TWENTY LODGES

It was no time for negotiations. Not a time for anything, in fact, but silence and obscurity on my part; so, with my companion, I sought the seclusion of Sitting Bull's tepee, where we spent the night in fitful and unrefreshing slumber. Early in the morning, at the first faint dawn of day, I was awakened by a call from Chief Gall, whom I joined in a walk about the camp. He informed me that the twenty lodges he had promised me had silently taken their departure during the night, and that I would find them in the evening, encamped about twenty miles down the Milk River. He said that five women and nine children belonging to the party, but who had no horses, had remained behind, and desired to ride in my wagon. He also informed me that Strong Hand would return with me to Poplar Creek. Accordingly, as soon as breakfast was over, we hitched up the mules, and were only too glad to get away from a place, where, to say the least, our experience had been very unpleasant. Strong Hand was returning afoot, and at his suggestion, I loaned him my horse, to enable him to traverse the river bottoms in quest of deer. The women and children climbed into the wagon with their meagre effects, and we began moving out of the camp, Strong Hand riding just in advance of the mules, while I occupied a seat with the driver. We had reached the outskirts of the camp, and were nearing the crossing of Frenchman's Creek, which was bordered on either side by a dense growth of willows, when I saw a number of warriors rapidly approaching us from the camp, each one carrying, in addition to his rifle, a stout club. From this I knew that they were what they call soldiers, corresponding to our police.

They called to Strong Hand to halt, but instead of obeying, he put whip to his horse and quickly disappeared through the willows at the crossing, but not before one of the Indians, a son of the noted Chief, Black Moon, had raised his rifle and sent a bullet flying after him.

Black Moon Wi Sapa (c. 1821–March 1, 1893) was a Miniconjou Lakota leader. At least one source states Black Moon's wife, daughter and son were killed at Wounded Knee.—Ed. 2018

My soldier friend, being unacquainted with Indian customs, supposed that we were sure enough attacked, and for an instant, lost his presence of mind, and was about to lash the mules into a run, in the mad hope of escaping from the savages in a ponderous government wagon, drawn by four equally ponderous draught mules. I snatched the lines from his hand, and reined in the mules, in the meantime begging Day not to get excited, and to put down that whip. He recovered himself instantly, when I handed him the lines and told him to hold the mules, and jumping to the ground, I ran directly to the brave who had fired the shot. I assumed a fearless demeanor which I did not feel, and demanded what was the matter. He waved me angrily away, repeating, "It is not you! It is not you! That man on your horse I wanted. He is himself a soldier of our band, and long ago he broke my arm with a blow from his club, when I had broken one of our customs , by flushing a herd of buffalo; now he has broken a law by leaving camp without our consent, and I proposed to retaliate, but he is gone, and now you go!" I obeyed with alacrity, while the warriors turned slowly back to their camp. We were clear of them at last, and right glad we were to know it.

It was nearly dark when we came up with the twenty lodges sent on ahead by Chief Gall. Strong Hand was there with plenty of good venison, and laughing heartily at the morning episode, which he explained more fully, and acknowledged that the principle reason for borrowing my horse' was now apparent. We returned in safety to Fort Buford, where, I hope, with a pardonable degree of pride, I turned over to Major Brotherton the first fruits of my labor, twenty lodges of the hostile Sioux, and submitted an official report to be forwarded to General Terry, of this, my second visit to the camp of Sitting Bull.

I remained in Buford five days, preparing for my third trip, and believing the work to have progressed to a period where I might find it necessary to extend, indefinitely, my stay in the camp, I determined to take with me someone to act in the capacity of courier, which would enable me to send a report back to Major Brotherton. For this purpose I chose the post interpreter, George Mulligan, with whom I started on about the 20th of November, reaching Camp Poplar Creek, sixty-five miles west of Buford, in two days.

At this place is situated, beside the small garrison of troops, the Fort Peck, or Poplar Creek Agency for the Yanktonai Sioux, who, at that time, numbered, all told, about two thousand five hundred. These were professedly friendly Indians, who belonged properly to the Agencies on the lower Missouri, in Dakota. There is a bit of history connected with the location of these Indians in Montana, that I intend to make the subject of a chapter in a work that I expect to publish in the near future. From these people I received important information, to the effect that an Indian had arrived from Sitting Bull's Camp, who reported that an open rupture had occurred between Chief Gall and Sitting Bull, occasioned by the discovery by some of the adherents of Sitting Bull, that Chief Gall had instigated the desertion of the twenty lodges, who had gone with me to Buford, and concealment being no longer possible, Chief Gall, characteristically prompt in action, had leaped into the midst of the camp, and publicly called upon all who acknowledged him as their Chief, to separate themselves from the followers of Sitting Bull, and prepare immediately to follow him to Fort Buford. It was a bold thing to do, and the first time in the history of the reign of Sitting Bull, that his authority had been set at defiance. It was clearly a test of supremacy, and Chief Gall came off victorious, taking away from Sitting Bull fully two-thirds of the entire band, with whom he proceeded direct to Poplar Creek, where I awaited his arrival, which took place on the 25th.

Sitting Bull was now left with only about three hundred lodges, altogether too small a force to expect to successfully defend themselves against even their Indian enemies. I, therefore, after a long talk with Chief Gall, determined to push right on to Woody Mountain and press negotiations while circumstances seemed to promise success. There were grave uncertainties, however, as to how I would be received. Their troubles, not the least of which, in the estimation of his adherents, was the decline of Sitting Bull's power, might all be dated from my first visit to their camp, and my friend, the Gall, would not be there to protect me from the vengeance of the desperate savages. One thing was certain, Sitting Bull had by this time divined my real purpose, and any attempt at concealment would be futile. But the work could not be done by proxy, so I had to go on, or sneak back to Buford and own up that I was afraid to go on with the work, and subject myself to the tantalizing "I told you so" of the knowing one, whose name is legion, and whose home is everywhere. Accordingly, after arranging with The Gall to remain with his band at Poplar Creek till my return, and sending a report to Major Brotherton, by an Indian, I continued, accompanied by Mulligan, to Woody Mountain.

Winter had already set in. and we had a cold ride across the hundred and ten mile prairie, reaching the Woody Mountain Trading Post on the 27th of November, where we learned that Sitting Bull's camp was distant only eighteen miles. Major Crozier of the Dominion forces, was in command of the small garrison of Mounted Police, stationed at the Trading Post, and at his suggestion,

I remained at the Post, and sent word, by an Indian, to Sitting Bull, to meet me there with all of his leading warriors, and with a view to putting them in good humor, I purchased from the trader a large quantity of provisions, which I had cooked, and prepared a sumptuous feast for them, which fact being conveyed to them by the Indian courier, they were not slow to respond. Sitting Bull met me with a slight exhibition of friendliness, evidently reluctantly assumed. Being deprived of the counsel and support of Chief Gall, he was at a loss what to do. Constitutionally a coward, fears for his own personal safety caused him to waver and withhold his consent to come in with me at once, and then, too, he was only human, and doubtless, coward though he was, his mind was stirred with other considerations than personal fear. His exalted position as Patriarch of a people, who, in his opinion, were the greatest nation on earth, was fast slipping away from him. It had been the boast of his life that he would never be dependent upon the hated white man. Time and again he had met them in battle, and had always been the victor. Must he at last, in this tame, humiliating manner, surrender himself, and become a prisoner in the hands of an hereditary foe? Who can tell how fierce the struggle of that moment? The mental anguish endured, while he revolved these, to him mighty questions, in his mind? What wonder that he hesitated, and asked a few more days to think and talk with his people about it? I explained to him fully, that his surrender must be virtually unconditional; the only thing guaranteed was that their lives should be spared. I was free, however, to express my opinion that they would be eventually treated as other Agency Indians, and promising to wait ten days for a decision, and apprehending that Mulligan was doing too much talking on his own account, I dispatched him, with a report of progress, to Major Brotherton. During the following ten days, from the first to the tenth of December, I visited the camp three times, staying overnight the first time with Sitting Bull, the second time with No Neck, and the third time with Black Bull, using every argument and persuasion at my command, to induce them to return with me to Buford, and having a better command of the Sioux than I have of English, I do believe I waxed really eloquent, for while talking to a small assembly in Black Bull's lodge, that Chief confessed that my words, while describing their distressed, hunted condition, and the hopelessness of their children's future, had moved him to tears, something never before accomplished by a white man.

On the morning of the tenth, I made an appointment to meet Sitting Bull and his warriors in the Trader's Store, at Woody Mountain, there to receive his final decision. Accordingly, about noon they were assembled and ready for the council, at which, by my request, Major Crozier was present, and gave me all the aid in

26

his power; but not till he withdrew from the council, did I finally succeed, about two o'clock p.m., in getting a promise from Sitting Bull and all of his followers, to raise camp the next morning, the 11th of December, 1880, and move with me toward the Missouri River. As soon as they had thus decided, most of them departed at once for their camp, to prepare for the morning's march, Sitting Bull among the number; I having promised to follow in time to reach the camp that night, and sleep in Bull's lodge. Five or six of the warriors remained in the store to do some trading. One of them was Black Bull, or as he was called by the Indians, Lame Brule, a chief noted for bravery, another was the son of Black Moon, who, on the occasion of my second visit to the camp, had fired a shot at Strong Hand.

After purchasing as much food as I could conveniently pack on my horse, and sending a dispatch by a Cree half-breed to Major Brotherton, I started on Sitting Bull's trail to the camp, eighteen miles away. The snow was deep, and the temperature unusually cold, but my horse was too heavily burdened to admit of fast riding, so I was jogging along at an easy pace, and keeping a sharp lookout from force of habit, and had gone about nine miles, when I discovered an Indian following after me, at the highest rate of speed, and frantically beckoning me to stop. I halted, and awaited his approach. It was Black Bull; he had brought me a dispatch, signed by Fred Cadd, the trader, and endorsed by Major Crozier, which read as follows:

"Your life is threatened; return at once! Black Bull will explain." which he did, by informing me that soon after I had left the store, perhaps forty-five minutes, Black Moon's son gave the trader a deer skin, in exchange for which he asked for a quantity of flour, sugar and coffee. The same having been weighed out to him, he was dissatisfied with the trade, claiming that he was being cheated, (which was doubtless true,) and the trader refusing, either to give him more or return the deer skin, he flew into a rage and attempted to shoot the trader on the spot: but being frustrated in his purpose, (Black Bull modestly refrained from stating the fact, which I afterwards learned, that it was he who had saved the trader's life,) he declared that though they had cheated him out of his deer skin, and prevented his killing the trader, they could not cheat him of vengeance, for he knew of one white man who was in his power, and whose hot blood should melt the frozen snow, before the sun went down, and leaving the store, he mounted his horse and rode furiously away by a trail nearly parallel with the one taken by me, and the natural conclusion reached by all, was that he meant me, and this was the opinion of Black Bull, who urged me to return with him to the Trading Post, believing, he said, that I would be waylaid and murdered before I reached the camp. This was perplexing; success apparently almost within my grasp, and now this unexpected difficulty presents itself. What should I do? I had given my word to be in camp that night, and I had the promise of Sitting Bull and all his leading warriors to start for the American lines in the morning. If I failed to reach the camp that night, they, of course, would fail to move in the morning, and our agreement would be void, and total failure would probably result. Better go ahead and be killed, than go back and be laughed at.

Penciling on the back of the dispatch, my determination to go on at all hazard, I sent Black Bull back with it, while I slowly and thoughtfully pursued my way to the camp, closely scanning every ravine and bunch of poplars or sage bush, that might serve as a hiding place for the enraged warrior; but nothing unusual occurred, and I reached the camp in safety. Supper was waiting me in Sitting Bull's lodge, which was to be my home for the next ten days. While smoking a pipe with the Chief, after supper, I told him what I had heard of the difficulty at the trader's store. He said that a little while before my arrival, the Black Moon's son had returned to the camp, his horse wet with sweat and apparently exhausted, which fact was noticed and commented on by several, but having made no statement, they had supposed that the proposed movement in the morning was all that agitated his mind. While we were yet discussing the matter, a little girl came into the tepee, and said that her father wanted me to come to his lodge, and immediately went out again, when Sitting Bull told me that that was Black Moon's son's little daughter. Then it was the enraged warrior himself, who wanted to see me. What for? There was no use trying to evade a meeting; I might as well go and take my medicine at once, and be done with it; so taking my rifle, I followed the little girl to her father's lodge. Going in, I found the warrior apparently in the best of good humor, filling a pipe, preparatory to a smoke. He motioned me to a seat, where his squaw served me with a large hot pancake and a cup of coffee, and while I was eating, supposing that I knew nothing of his encounter with the trader, he told me all about it, evidently with a desire to conceal nothing, not even his threat of vengeance, and concluded exultingly, while his countenance actually glowed with savage satisfaction, that *he had kept his word.*

While my heart was saddened by the thought that someone's life had been sacrificed to the avaricious greed of an Indian trader, yet I was certainly rejoiced to know, that after all, he had not chosen me as the object of his vengeance.

Several weeks afterwards, I learned that the mail, due in Woody Mountain that evening, had failed to arrive, and that some days later, fragments of human remains dragged around and scattered about by wolves, with shreds of clothing, revealed the fact that the mail carrier had been killed.

The warrior then explained that he had sent for me to tell me these things himself, and assure me that I need have no fears for my own safety, as far as he was concerned. It was his turn to be surprised, when I told him how I had heard all about it before I got to the camp, and when I mentioned the name of Black Bull as being the one who brought me the dispatch, he gnashed his teeth, as he said, "Only for him, *I would have got the real offender.*"

Early the next morning found us moving toward the Missouri River; Black Bull and the others having returned from the Trading Post during the night.

Having barely horses enough to pack their effects, nearly all the able bodied warriors and squaws were afoot. The order of march being, First, three mounted warriors, who moved out about one hour in advance of the main body of warriors, one keeping to the proposed line of march, the other two acting as flankers, observing a distance of about one mile from the center guide; next in line of march, and. immediately preceding the main body, were about fifty warriors afoot, and armed for action, who moved, however, without any more display of military order than would a herd of so many cattle. Then followed the camp proper, the squaws leading and driving the ponies, all heavily laden with camp equipage, not even the little colts were exempt from burden, and all in an indescribable state of disorder. Bringing up the rear, was a guard of about seventy-five mounted warriors. From this company, at intervals of about a mile, all along the line of march, small detachments of five or six were sent ahead, riding rapidly on either flank, until they reached a point a mile or two in advance of the main column, when, taking a position on some convenient hill, they would dismount, sit down in the snow, and fill a pipe for a smoke, while their horses were free to forage in the snow for the nutritious buffalo grass. Here they would remain until the rear guard came up, when they would rejoin them.

In the meantime, another party of flankers had gone out, and so on, all day long. Our progress was necessarily slow, and we made only about an average of twelve miles a day. As to myself, I rode at will, sometimes with the advance guard, and sometimes with the main body, and again with the rear guard; always speaking words of encouragement to the feeble, and cheering the little ones with a prospect of good things, when we should get to Fort Buford. The weather was not cold for the first week, so there was but little suffering from that source; but we found no game, save an occasional jack rabbit, and the scant supply of food was nearly exhausted, and there was consequent suffering from hunger, and like the Israelites of old, they began to murmur.

On our third day's march, I was riding by the side of Sitting Bull, just in the rear of the main body, when my name was called by a young warrior, a member of a flanking party, who were resting on a little hill by the wayside, who stood up and beckoned me to come to him. Sitting Bull rode with me to the group, where we halted, and I asked the young man what he wanted. He seemed embarrassed, and stood for nearly a minute, without replying, holding the muzzle of his rifle in his hands, while the butt rested on the ground. At last he said, looking at me, while his lips quivered and his voice trembled with savage emotion, "Where are you taking these people to?" "To Fort Buford," (*O-kee-ja-ta*) I replied. "Then why don't you feed them, don't you know that they are hungry?" said he. I was about to reply, but Sitting. Bull, realizing the situation, adroitly placed himself between me and the speaker, and while indicating by signs, that I should move on, he himself engaged the young man in conversation, and when a little later, he overtook me, he simply said, "The young man's heart is bad; his little sister is crying for food." Only for the intervention of Sitting Bull, I have no doubt but the young man would have attempted my life. On other occasions, I narrowly escaped death at the hands of the turbulent and ungovernable savages; but as this is not intended as a history of my own adventures, but of the surrender of Sitting Bull, I will hasten on.

Our course was down the Rock Creek Valley for the first seven days, when we turned east and crossed over to the Porcupine Creek, which we followed for three days, to its confluence with the Milk River, distant only three miles from the great Missouri. Here we found buffalo in great numbers; there being within a radius of thirty miles, no less than thirty-five thousand. Here I determined to improve the opportunity for getting in a good Supply of food and robes for the destitute Indians, and accordingly advised the head men to choose a camping ground, with a view to greater security against their Indian enemies.

That evening, after we had gone into camp, and everybody had satisfied their hunger by a bounteous supply of buffalo meat, I called a council of the chiefs, and asked them to select three braves to go at once with me as delegates, on a visit to Fort Buford, my object being, as I told them, to convince them that their treatment by Major Brotherton would be good. I desired, also, that they receive confirmation from the lips of Major Brotherton himself, of all the representations that I had made them, concerning their surrender. Sitting Bull then called for three volunteers to go with me; but for a long time there was no response.

Finally, after the assembled warriors had smoked their pipes in silence for full twenty minutes, causing a feeling of portentous gloom to pervade the atmosphere of the council lodge, suddenly, a tall, athletic warrior sprang to his feet, and taking a position in the center of the lodge, and facing me, gesticulating excitedly, he said: "I am toe Patriarch Crow! My kinsmen, you all know me: you have never known me as the friend of the white man; you know that I have always hastened into the thickest of the fight, when the white man was our foe, nor did I withhold my hand when they cried for mercy, and the fact that we are now on our way to Fort Buford, to sue for peace, was not of my choosing; but when, eleven days ago, the chiefs of this band decided upon this course, that day I forgot that the white man was my enemy; that day, Patriarch Crow, the white man's enemy, died, and today, Patriarch Crow, the white man's friend lives, and he it is who speaks these words, and since volunteers were never lacking for deeds of war, neither shall they be lacking when called for a mission of peace. I go with my friend to Buford. Who will be the next to speak?"

He then advanced, and shaking hands with me, sat down by my side, great drops of sweat rolling off his face. Though a leading warrior, and always foremost in battle, he was never before known to make a public speech, and I had his assurance that I was the first white man with whom he had ever shaken hands. He afterwards proved of invaluable service, but has since died at Standing Rock Agency, Dakota, where he was known, through the misinterpretation of his name, as the Crow King. Two others

32

immediately volunteered, and the next morning, leaving the camp, where they were, for the first time in five years, in the midst of buffalo, I started with them for Buford, where we arrived on Christmas Eve, December 24, 1880.

Crow King, also known as Medicine Bag That Burns, Burns The Medicine Bag or simply Medicine Bag, played an important role in the defeat of Custer at the Little Bighorn. He died in 1884.—Ed. 2018

DISASTROUS RESULTS AVERTED

On our way we had stopped at Poplar Creek, where I had an interview with Chief Gall, who informed me that many of his followers were becoming demoralized through the machinations of some of the so-called friendly Chiefs at the Agency, who wanted them not to go to Fort Buford to surrender, but to be enrolled as members of their bands at that Agency; dwelling upon the fact, as an inducement, that the Poplar Creek Agency was much nearer the buffalo range than the Agencies below in Dakota. He further informed me, that unless measures were taken to restrict the Agency Chiefs, when the time came to continue the march to Buford, many of his band would refuse to leave Poplar Creek. All these facts I reported to Major Brotherton, and advised that the two companies stationed at Poplar Creek, be re-enforced by at least five companies, which was accordingly done. Three companies being sent from Fort Keogh, Montana, and two from Buford, and all commanded by Major Guido Ilges.

Prussian-born Guido Joseph Julius Ilges (1835-1918) was a brevet lieutenant-colonel for actions at the Wilderness and Spotsylvania in the Civil War (Fort Benton blog).

My object in having the garrison at Poplar Creek reinforced, was to overawe the Agency Chiefs and prevent their interference with the hostiles; but being detained with the delegates longer in Buford than I had anticipated, Major Ilges, with the reinforcements, reached Camp Poplar Creek ahead of me, and immediately undertook a little work on his own account, and for his own glory, which, only for the prompt and decided action, first, of Chief Gall, and afterwards of Patriarch Crow, would have undone all the work that I had thus far accomplished. He demanded the immediate and unconditional surrender of Chief Gall and his band. This was in the afternoon of about the ninth day of January, 1881, and I reached Poplar Creek with the Patriarch Crow and his two companions that night. Chief Gall heard of my return, and early in the morning, came over from his camp, which was situated in the woods across the Missouri River, crossing on the ice, to see me, and as he said, to present me with the pony he rode, a splendid black mare. He was proceeding to tell me how Major Ilges had ordered his surrender, when looking toward the military camp, we saw the entire command mounted, and in line with two pieces of artillery, and moving toward the river, in the direction of Gall's camp. Here was a splendid opportunity for a repetition of the Custer Massacre. Not more than four hundred soldiers going out to do battle with fully that many Indians, who had the advantage of being afoot, and protected by heavy timber and dense underbrush, while the soldiers had to advance, mounted, in plain view of the Indians, across an open field of ice.

"Quick! Mount and go!" said I. "You must reach your camp before those soldiers are within rifle range, and no matter what happens, don't you allow one of your warriors to lift a gun! And as soon as possible, display a white flag, and surrender. I will take you to Buford, nevertheless."

He threw himself on to the back of the beautiful black pony and was away with the swiftness of a deer. Calling Patriarch Crow, who had been standing a little way off, I climbed with him to the top of the trader's store, from which point we could watch the movement of the troops, and had a plain view of the timber in which the Indians were encamped. Our interest was centered on the movements of Chief Gall, for everything depended on his ability to reach the camp, which was only about a mile and a half distant, before the Indians were aroused by the approach of the troops. Fortunately for the troops, he got there in time, but none too soon, for he had no sooner disappeared in the timber that hid the camp, than the troops formed in line of battle, wheeled the two pieces of artillery into position, and without making any attempt whatever to hold a parley with the Indians, with a view to a peaceful surrender, immediately opened fire on the camp, firing volley after volley into the camp, from the small arms, and at the same time shelling the woods with the field pieces. I have never ceased to wonder at the almost superhuman power exerted by Chief Gall over his people, which enabled him to hold them from returning the attack, and I wonder more that he restrained himself; but he is a man of strong determination, and having made up his mind to quit the war path, nothing could turn him from his purpose. He soon appeared, emerging from the timber, in the very face of the troops, waving a piece of white muslin at the end of a pole, when the firing ceased, and the soldiers took possession of the camp. Not a shot had been fired by the Indians, and though repeated volleys had been fired into the camp by the soldiers, only one squaw was killed and one warrior wounded. When the news reached the States, it was a battle, and Major Ilges got his full mead of praise.

The attack upon the camp was made early in the morning, at a time when many of the warriors were taking their ponies out into the hills to graze. These heard the heavy firing and attempted to return, but finding the camp in the possession of the troops, fled westwardly, up the Missouri Valley, in the direction of Sitting Bull's camp. Our position on the roof of the store, enabled us to see the fugitives, as, one after another, they flew past the openings in the timber that skirted the banks of the river. This was an important discovery.

These Indians would undoubtedly go to Sitting Bull's camp, and being ignorant of the real situation, their report would certainly stampede the entire outfit, and they would all go back across the Canadian border, in which case I might abandon all hope of effecting their surrender. Prompt and energetic action alone would avert the threatened misfortune.

Patriarch Crow, by the kind treatment he had received at Fort Buford, was completely won over to the side of the Government, and I knew that I could rely on him in this emergency; and he proved himself worthy of my confidence. He saw the difficulty, and understood as well asI1, what the result would be, unless something was done, and, therefore, when I urged him to fly to the camp and do all he could to prevent a stampede, he was ready to go, and though he was evidently indignant at the action of the troops, immediately mounted his horse, and after receiving an assurance from me, that I would follow as soon as circumstances would permit, he departed, saying, that I would either find the camp or his dead body at the mouth of Milk River.

SITTING BULL SOON FOLLOWS

I remained three days at Poplar Creek, assisting in the removal of Gall's band to Fort Buford, transportation having been provided by an order from General Terry. The weather becoming intensely cold, there was much suffering among the women and children, many of them having their feet, hands and faces frozen; but all received most excellent care as soon as they arrived at Buford, and were placed under the care of Major Brotherton.

When I started again for Sitting Bull's camp, I went in a government sleigh, with the dauntless Day again as teamster, and this time I was accompanied by Mr. Charles Deihl [*sic*], of the Chicago Times.

Charles Sanford Diehl (1854 – 1946) was born in Maryland but grew up in Illinois. He was with the Times *for ten years under legendary publisher, Wilbur F. Storey. He was a manager for Associated Press in Chicago, San Francisco, and New York. One of his colleagues at the* Times *was John F. Finerty, who wrote an excellent memoir of his time with General Crook's division in 1876, including at the Battle of the Rosebud. See* On the Trail of Crazy Horse.*—Ed. 2018*

On the evening of the second day out from Poplar Creek, we stopped for the night in a deserted cabin in the woods by the river. Nearby, I found encamped three or four families, who had the day before left Sitting Bull's camp, from whom I received important information. They said that the fugitives had reached the camp and spread the news of the attack by the troops at Poplar Creek, alarming the Indians, who, with Sitting Bull in the lead, began a hasty retreat to the north, so that the whole tribe was in motion, when Patriarch Crow rode furiously into their midst, calling loudly for his four brothers and their friends to rally around him. He was quickly surrounded by an eager multitude, anxious to hear what he would say. He declared to them that the fugitives were cowards who had run without reason; that they had fled before they knew what the firing was about. He denounced them all for allowing their fears to get the better of their reason, and sarcastically inquired how many of them were wounded, and how many had been slain, defending the camp. He then declared that since not one of them

37

had had the courage to protest against this unreasonable, cowardly flight, therefore, not one of them was worthy of chieftainship. That whoever he might be, who had heretofore assumed that honor, he must now, and forever after, be silent; for the time had now come when the voice of the Patriarch Crow should be heard, and that he would be obeyed, none who knew him would doubt, and then calling upon all in whose hearts his words had found lodgment to follow him. He then rode rapidly to the head of the flying column, followed by all the warriors who had heard him and together, they compelled everyone to come back and re-occupy the camp they had so recently deserted.

The next act of Patriarch Crow, I suspect was prompted by his ambition to succeed permanently to the chieftainship, and believing that this could be more easily accomplished by destroying entirely the influence of Sitting Bull, and driving him back to Canada, which would leave him, Patriarch Crow, without a rival in that division of the tribe. Be that as it may, I could not be otherwise than well pleased with what he did, considering all the circumstances.

Early the next morning, the Patriarch Crow compelled Sitting Bull to remove his tepee to a small opening in the timber, three hundred yards away from the main camp, which being done, he then mounted his horse, and riding up and down through the camp, he called on all who were cowards, to remove their tepees to the opening with Sitting Bull, but those who were not cowards, should remain where they were. Forty-three families, all told, took their place in the opening, leaving about three hundred with Patriarch Crow, who then told Sitting Bull to go, and not to halt until he had crossed the Canadian border; and he went, and soon disappeared in the wind driven snows of the north. Patriarch Crow then commanded the initial movement toward Fort Buford, and encamped, where I met him in the evening, about three miles below the mouth of Milk River, they having made only about six miles on this first days' march under the new, self-appointed chief.

The march from that point to Fort Buford was uninterrupted, but was necessarily slow, in consequence of the deep snows and extreme cold weather. At a point thirty miles west of Wolf Point, I was met by a train of thirty government wagons and sleighs, sent out by Major Brotherton. These proved of valuable service, and greatly expedited our march, enabling us to reach Buford on about the tenth of February, where the hostiles under the Patriarch Crow, formally surrendered to Major Brotherton, and were placed, with the Chief Gall's band, in winter camp, to await transportation in the spring to Standing Rock Agency.

I now proposed to make one more trip to Woody Mountain, for Sitting Bull, but General Terry regarded the work as completed. All of the hostiles, with the exception of the small number of forty-three families, having surrendered, Sitting Bull was left without a following, and his power for evil being entirely destroyed, it was a matter of indifference to our government if he himself never came in, and this view was also held by General Sheridan. Therefore, no further steps were taken to induce him to surrender, save that I sent him word by an Indian, that he could follow his people to Fort Buford, where he would receive the same treatment received by them, and that I would be glad to have him do so, and this he finally did, arriving in Fort Buford in July, with about thirty-five families, a few families having remained, and still remain, in Canada; among the number, the intrepid Black Bull, and my old friend, The Lung, who chose to cast their fortunes with the Red River Half-Breeds of the north.

The other hostiles had previously been removed to Standing Rock, to which place we followed with Sitting Bull, whose subsequent history is a matter with which the public are acquainted.

E. H. ALLISON,

Scout, U. S. A.

THE END

Made in the USA
Middletown, DE
17 May 2024